BEAR FAIRY EDUCATION

Shapes Basic Geometry Workbook

Published by: BEAR FAIRY EDUCATION.
Interior Design by: Pani Palmer, Kentucky
Cover Design by: Pani Palmer, Kentucky

10 9 8 7 6 5 4 3 2 1
1. Workbook for Kids 2. Basic Early Learning Children Book
First Edition

TRIANGLE

COLOR THIS SHAPE RED

→

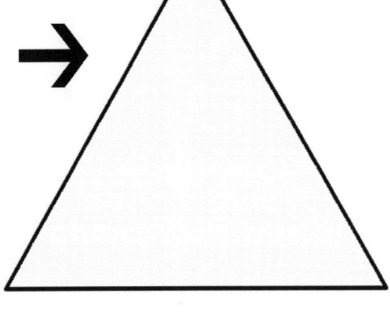

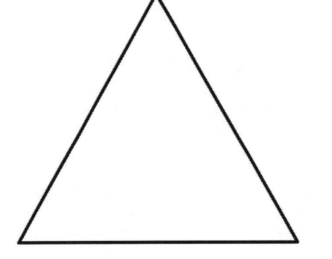

This shape is a triangle. It has ____ sides.

CIRCLE

COLOR THIS SHAPE GREEN

→

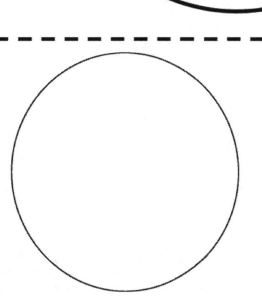

This shape is a circle. It has ____ sides.

RECTANGLE

COLOR THIS SHAPE BLUE

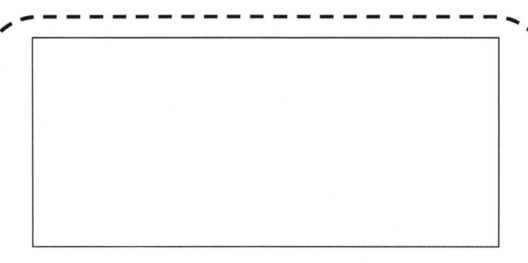

This shape is a rectangle. It has ____ sides.

OVAL

COLOR THIS SHAPE ORANGE

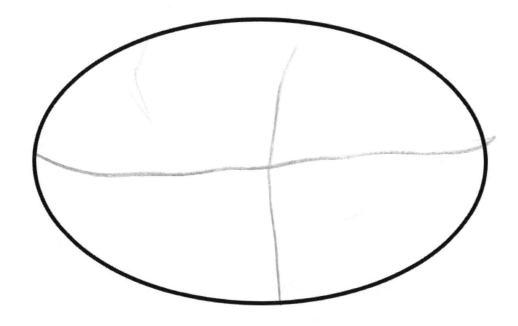

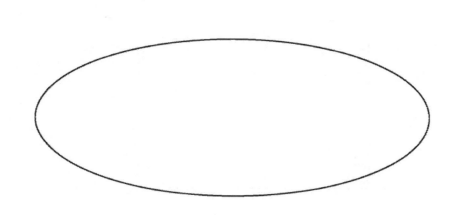

This shape is an oval. It has ____ sides.

SQUARE

COLOR THIS SHAPE BLACK

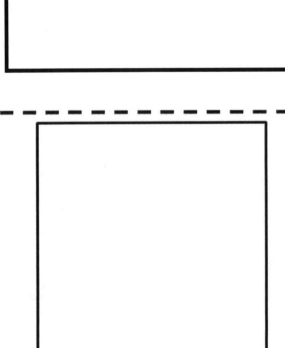

This shape is a square. It has ____ sides.

PENTAGON

COLOR THIS SHAPE BROWN

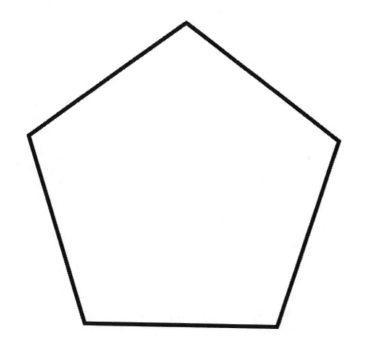

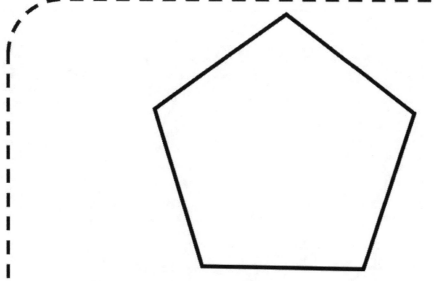

This shape is a PENTAGON. It has ____ sides.

HEXAGON

COLOR THIS SHAPE YELLOW

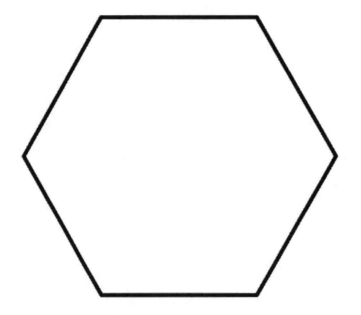

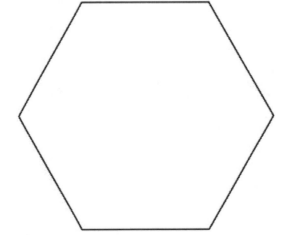

This shape is a hexagon. It has ____ sides.

RHOMBUS

COLOR THIS SHAPE RED

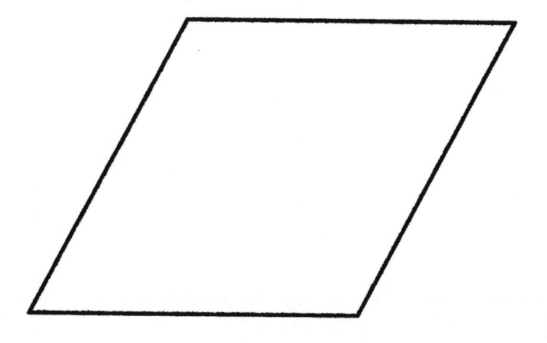

This shape is a rhombus. It has ____ sides.

TRAPEZOID

COLOR THIS SHAPE PURPLE

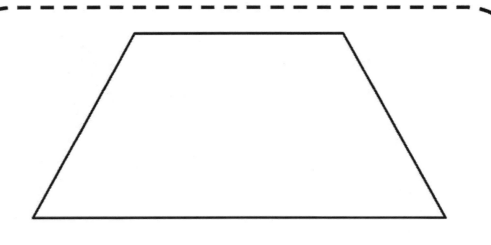

This shape is a trapezoid. It has ____ sides.

2D SHAPE ROLL & GRAPH

10						
9						
8						
7						
6						
5						
4						
3						
2						
1						

2D SHAPE ROLL & GRAPH

I graphed _____ squares.

I graphed _____ hexagons.

I graphed _____ circles.

I graphed _____ rhombi.

I graphed _____ triangles.

I graphed _____ trapezoids.

I graphed the most _____.

I graphed the least _____.

My favorite shape is _____.

COLOR THE SHIP
USING COLOR CODE BELOW

red   green   yellow   blue

EXERCISE 1

Color	Trace	Draw
Circle		
Square		
Triangle		
Rectangle		
Pentagon		

EXERCISE 2

Color	Trace	Draw
Pentagon		
Hexagon		
Octagon		
Rhombus		
Trapezium		

EXERCISE 3

LOOK AROUND AND DRAW THINGS THAT LOOK LIKE THE GIVEN SHAPE

Circle	Square
Triangle	Rectangle

ART GEOMETRY

DRAW A HOUSE BY USING GIVEN SHAPE AND COLOR IT

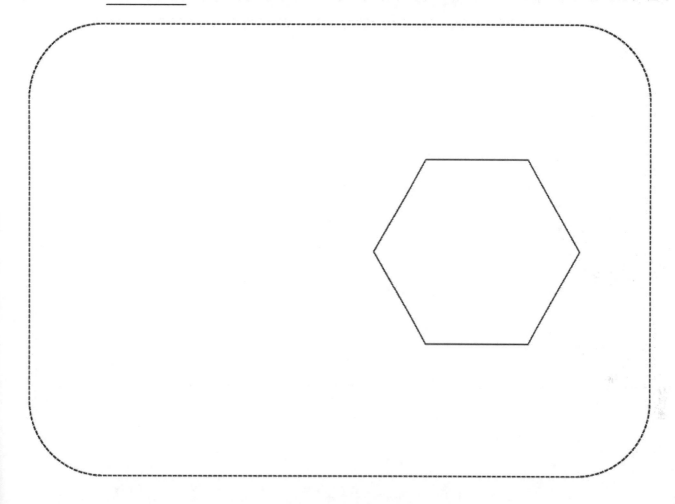

The shape I started with was a

_____

ART GEOMETRY

DRAW A <u>ROBOT</u> BY USING GIVEN SHAPE AND COLOR IT

The shape I started with was a

_____

ART GEOMETRY

DRAW A <u>CAT</u> BY USING GIVEN SHAPE AND COLOR IT

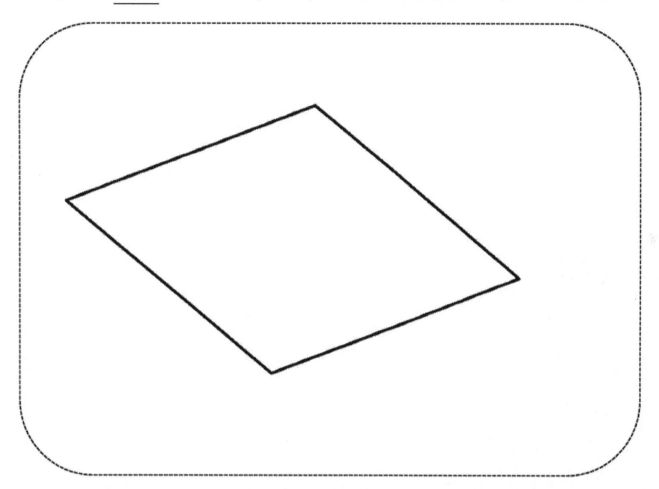

The shape I started with was a

_____

ART GEOMETRY

DRAW A <u>FOX</u> BY USING GIVEN SHAPE AND COLOR IT

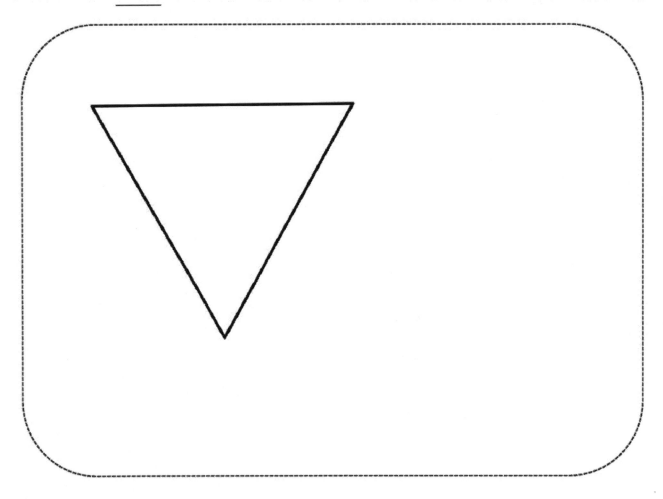

The shape I started with was a

_____

ART GEOMETRY

DRAW A <u>SPACESHIP</u> BY USING GIVEN SHAPE AND COLOR IT

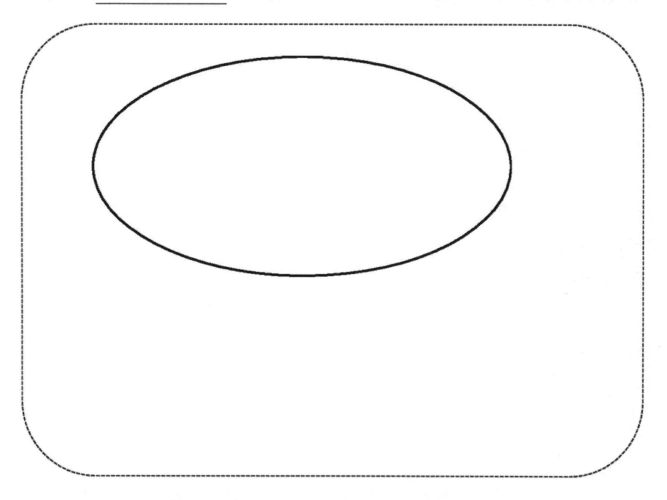

The shape I started with was a

_____

ART GEOMETRY

DRAW ANYTHING BY USING GIVEN SHAPE AND COLOR IT

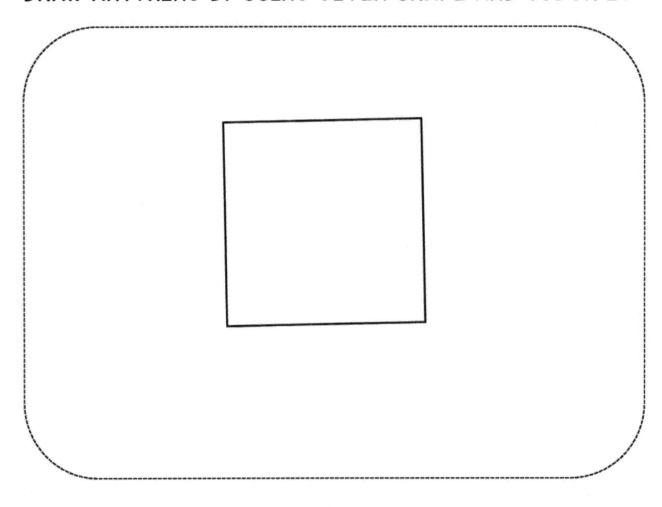

The shape I started with was a

_____

ART GEOMETRY

DRAW ANYTHING BY USING GIVEN SHAPE AND COLOR IT

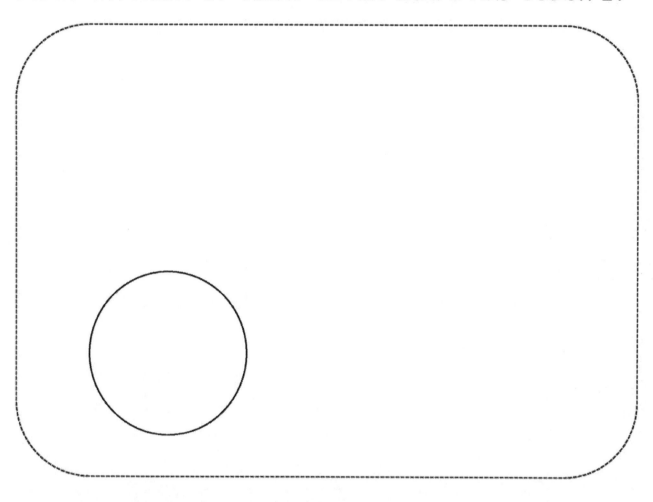

The shape I started with was a

_____

ART GEOMETRY

DRAW A TROPHY BY USING GIVEN SHAPE AND COLOR IT

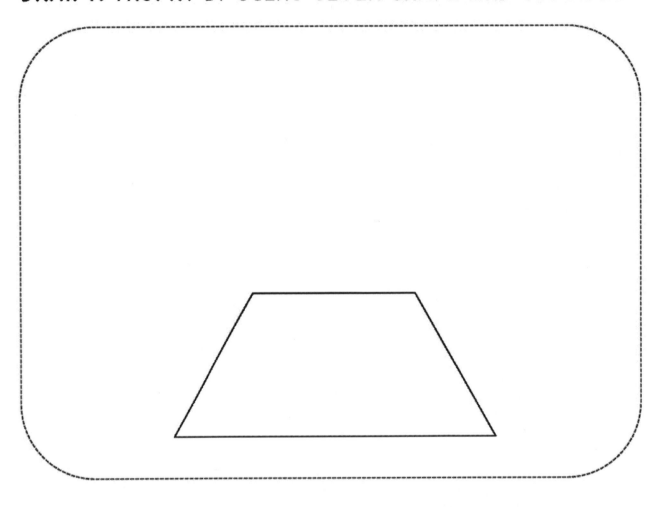

The shape I started with was a

_____

SPHERE

COLOR THIS SHAPE BLUE

This shape is a sphere.

CUBE

COLOR THIS SHAPE GREEN

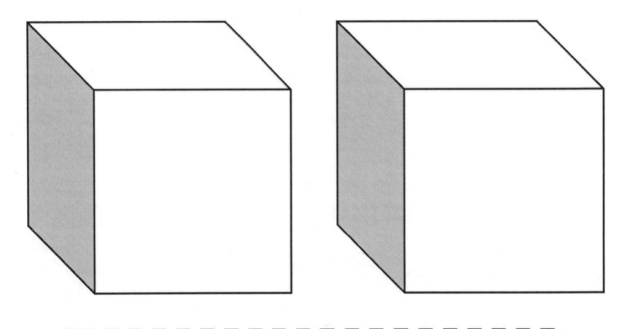

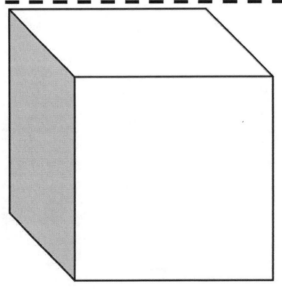

This shape is a cube.

PYRAMID

COLOR PYRAMIDS IN BROWN

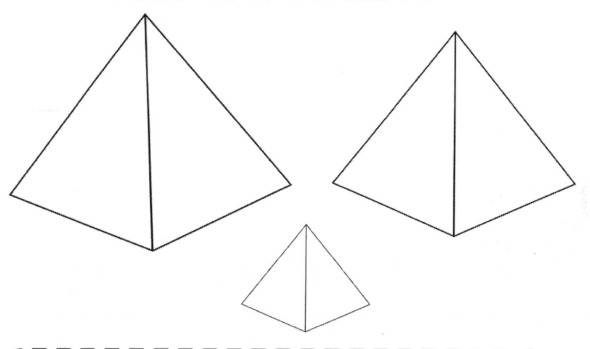

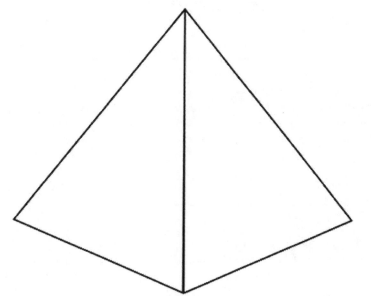

This shape is a pyramid.

RECTANGULAR

COLOR RECTANGULAR USING 2 COLORS

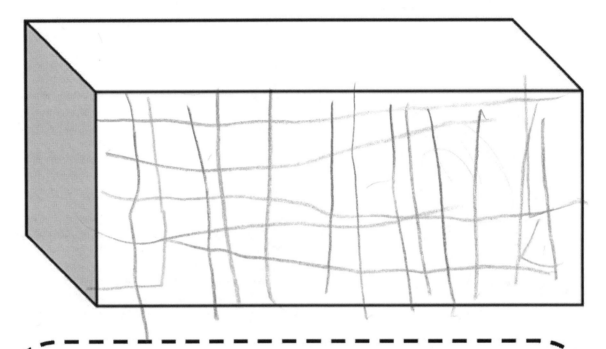

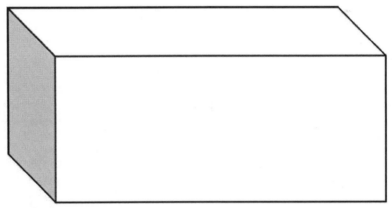

This shape is a rectangular prism.

CYLINDER

COLOR CYLINDER USING 3 COLORS

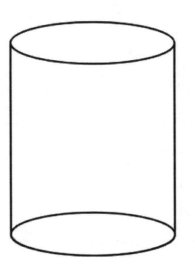

This shape is a cylinder.

CONE

COLOR CONE USING 2 COLORS

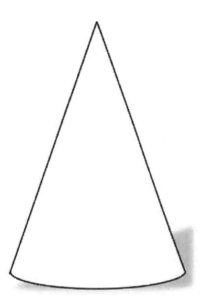 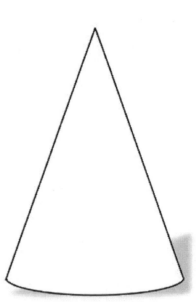

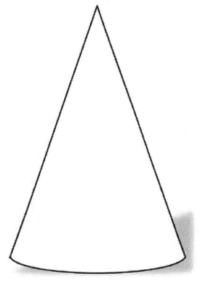

This shape is a cone.

EXERCISE 4

LOOK AROUND AND DRAW THINGS THAT LOOK LIKE THE GIVEN SHAPE

Sphere	Cylinder
Cube	Rectangular prism

EXERCISE 5

COLOR THE 3D SHAPE USING COLOR CODE

EXERCISE 6

COLOR THE 3D SHAPE USING COLOR CODE

Red | Blue | Yellow

EXERCISE 7

MARK IN THE BOX IF THE OBJECT CAN ROLL, SLIDE OR STACK

	Roll	Slide	Stack
Sphere	✔		
Cylinder			
Cube			
Cone			
Rectangular Prism			

EXERCISE 8

GRAPHING 3D SHAPES.

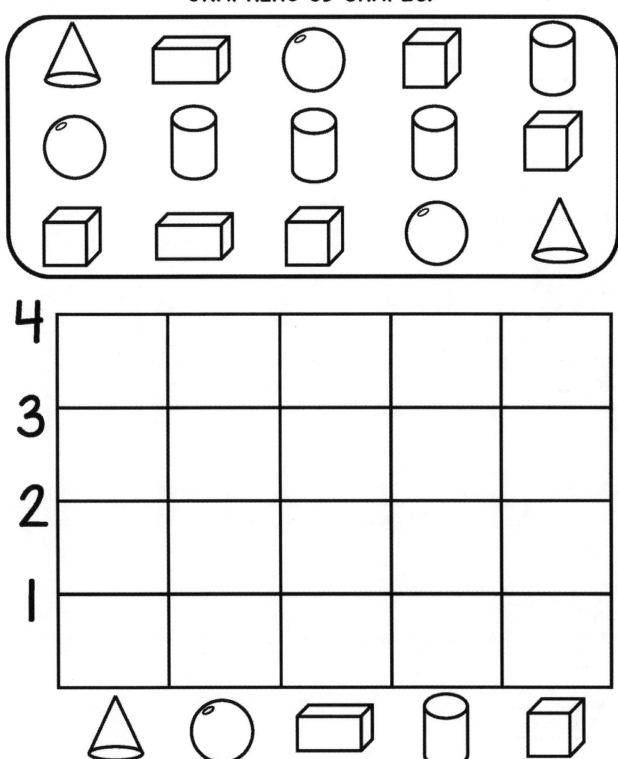

EXERCISE 9

COLOR THE SHAPES USING THE CODE BELOW.

ORANGE
Quadrilaterals

GREEN
Not Quadrilaterals

EXERCISE 10

COLOR THE SHAPES USING THE CODE BELOW.

BLUE	YELLOW
2D Shapes	3D Shapes

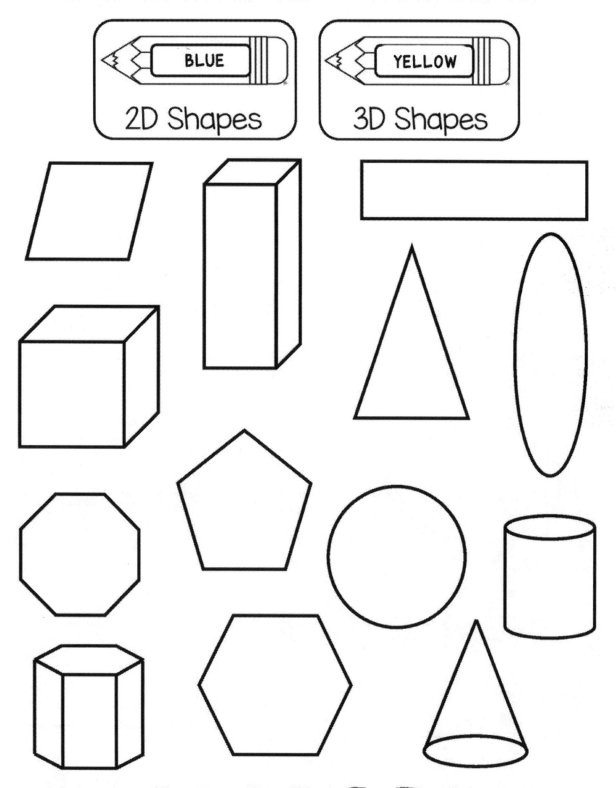

EXERCISE 11

 This is a circle.
Color the circle.

Trace the circle.

Trace the word.

Draw a picture of
something else that is
circle-shaped:

A ball is a circle.
Color the ball.

EXERCISE 12

 This is a square.
Color the square.

square

Trace the square   Trace the word.

Draw a picture of something else that is square-shaped:

This gift is a square.
Color the gift.

EXERCISE 13

△ This is a triangle.
Color the triangle.

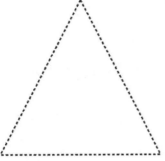

Trace the triangle.

triangle

Trace the word.

Draw a picture of something else that is triangle-shaped:

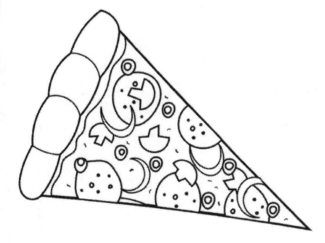

This slice of pizza is a triangle.
Color the pizza slice.

EXERCISE 14

This is a rectangle.
Color the rectangle.

Trace the rectangle.

rectangle

Trace the word.

Draw a picture of something else that is rectangle-shaped:

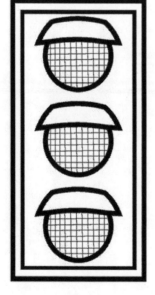

A traffic light is a rectangle.
Color the traffic light

EXERCISE 15

O **This is an oval.**
Color the oval.

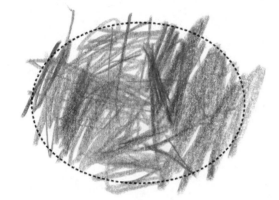

oval

Trace the oval.　Trace the word.

Draw a picture of something else that is oval-shaped:

An egg is an oval.
Color the egg.

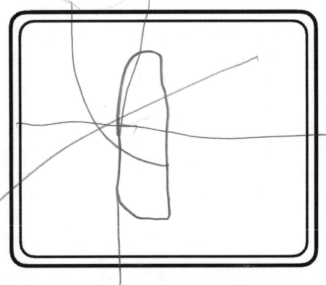

EXERCISE 16

 This is a heart.
Color the heart.

Trace the heart.

Trace the word.

Draw a picture of
something else that is
heart-shaped:

This leaf is heart-shaped.
Color the leaf.

EXERCISE 17

ORDER SHAPES FROM SMALLEST TO LARGEST
BY WRITING NUMBER INSIDE EACH SHAPE

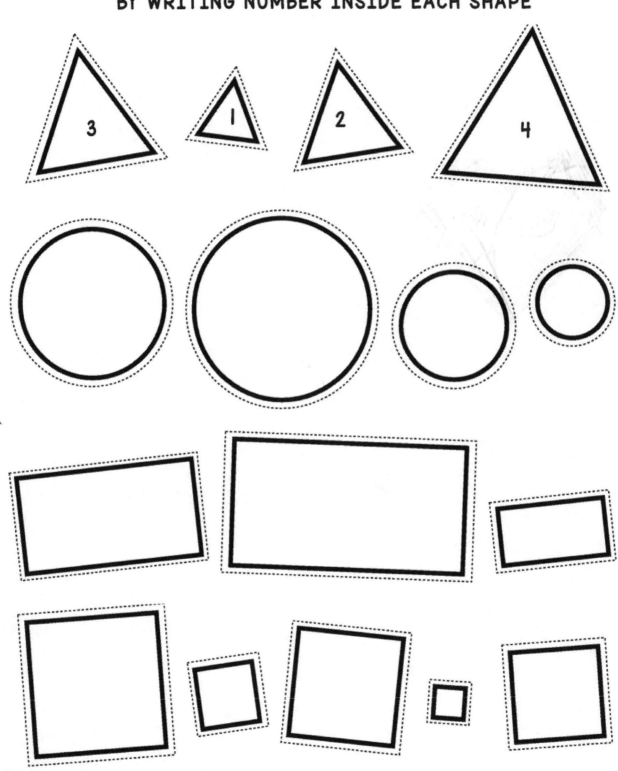

EXERCISE 18

DRAW A LINE TO MATCH EACH SHAPE WITH IT'S NAME

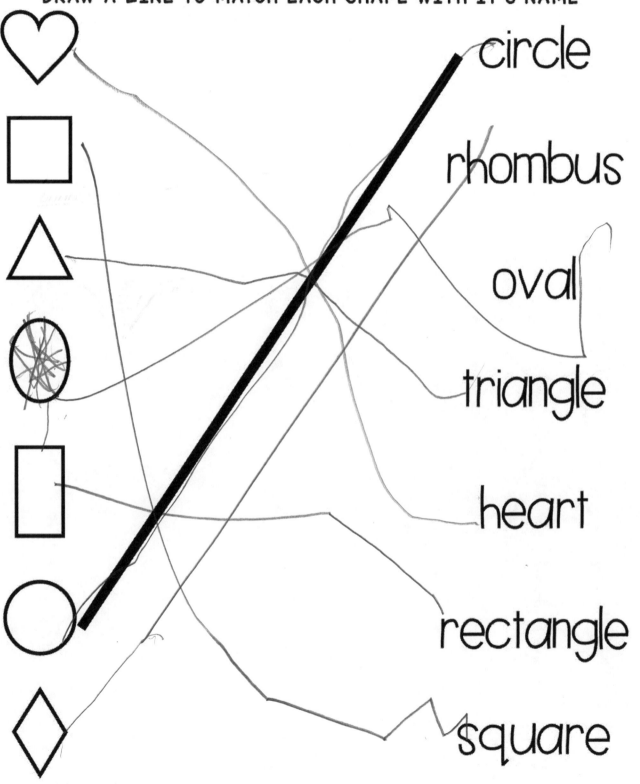

circle

rhombus

oval

triangle

heart

rectangle

square

EXERCISE 19

DRAW A LINE TO MATCH EACH SHAPE WITH AN OBJECT

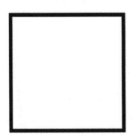
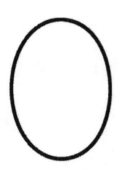
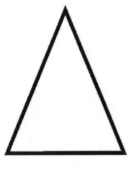
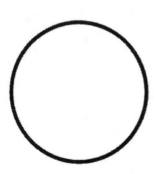

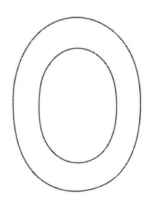

EXERCISE 20

TRACE THE SHAPES

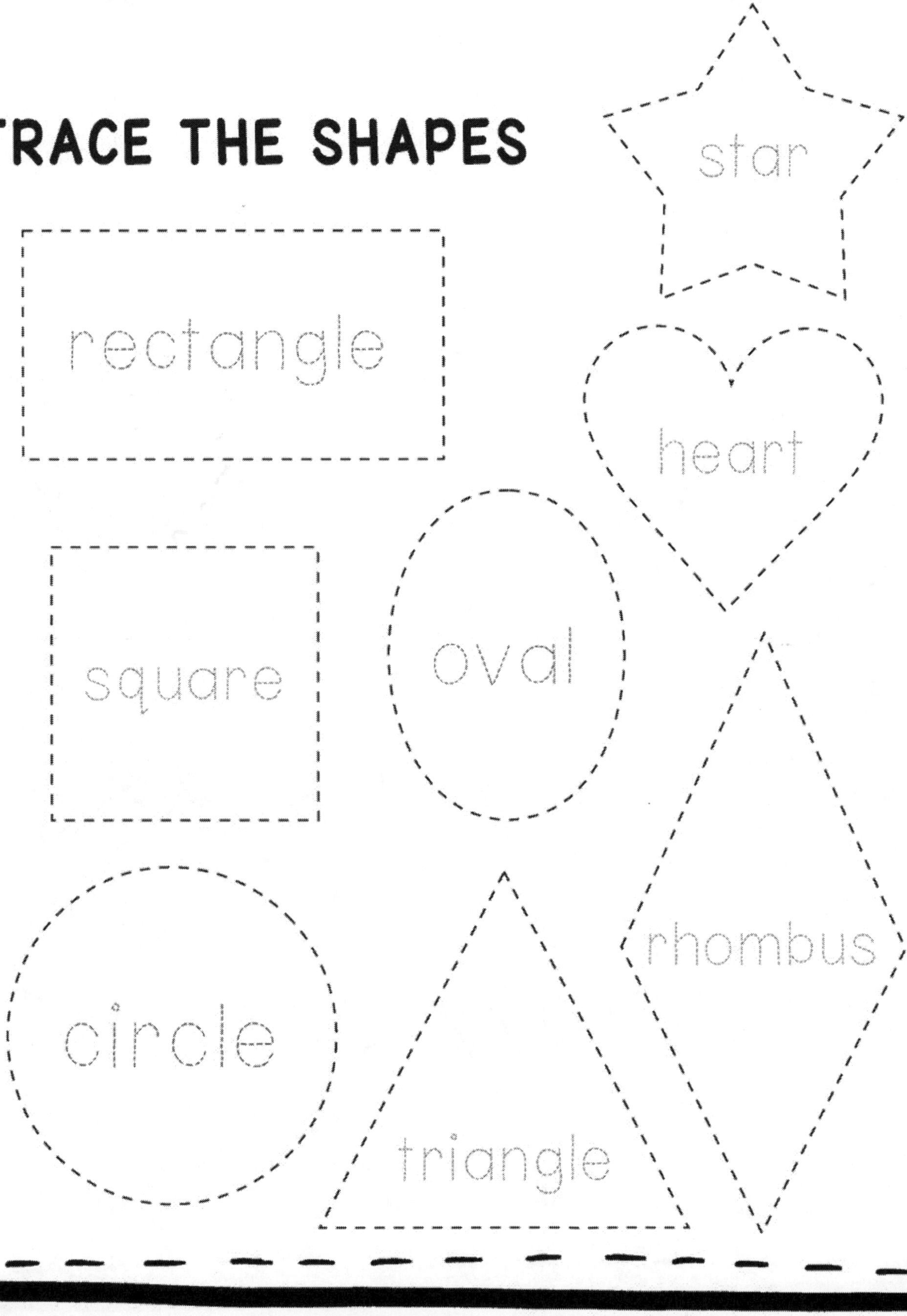

star

rectangle

heart

square

oval

circle

rhombus

triangle

EXERCISE 21

FIND CIRCLES AND COLOR THEM

EXERCISE 22

DRAW THE OTHER HALF OF EACH SHAPE

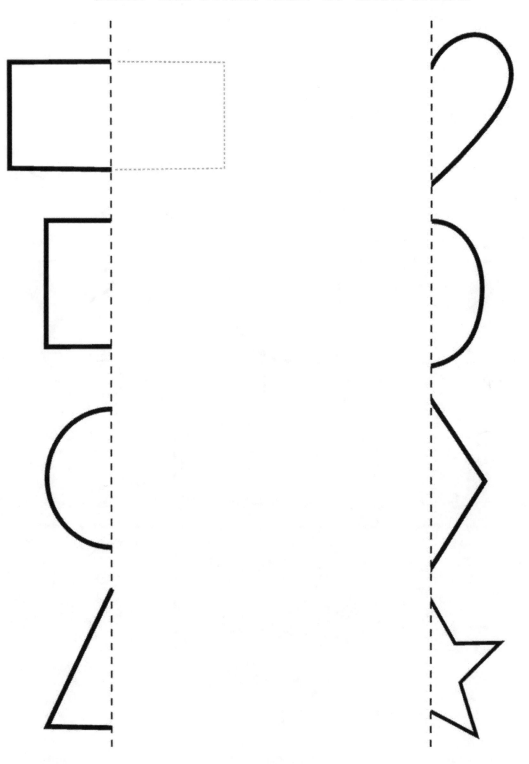

EXERCISE 23

COUNT EACH SHAPES IN THE BOX AND WRITE YOUR ANSWER.

EXERCISE 24

LOOK AT EACH ROW AND GUEST WHAT WILL BE THE NEXT SHAPE.
DRAW YOUR ANSWER INSIDE THE BOX.

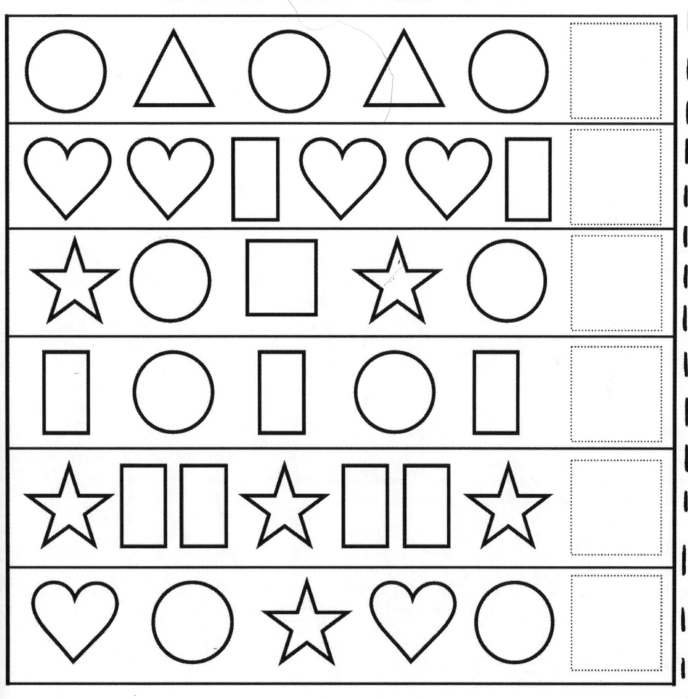

EXERCISE 25

FIND OVALS AND COLOR THEM ALL

EXERCISE 26

FIND HEARTS AND COLOR THEM ALl

EXERCISE 27

FIND TRIANGLES AND COLOR THEM ALL

EXERCISE 28

FIND PENTAGONS AND COLOR THEM ALL

EXERCISE 29

FIND HEXAGONS AND COLOR THEM ALL

CREATE YOUR OWN SHAPE

CREATE YOUR OWN SHAPE BY DRAWING AND COLORING IT.

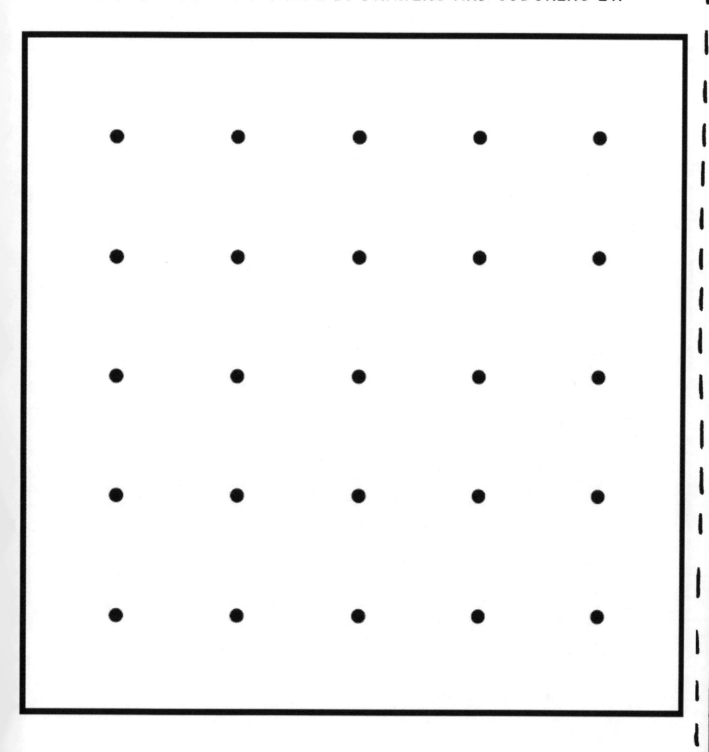

CREATE YOUR OWN SHAPE

CREATE YOUR OWN SHAPE BY DRAWING AND COLORING IT.

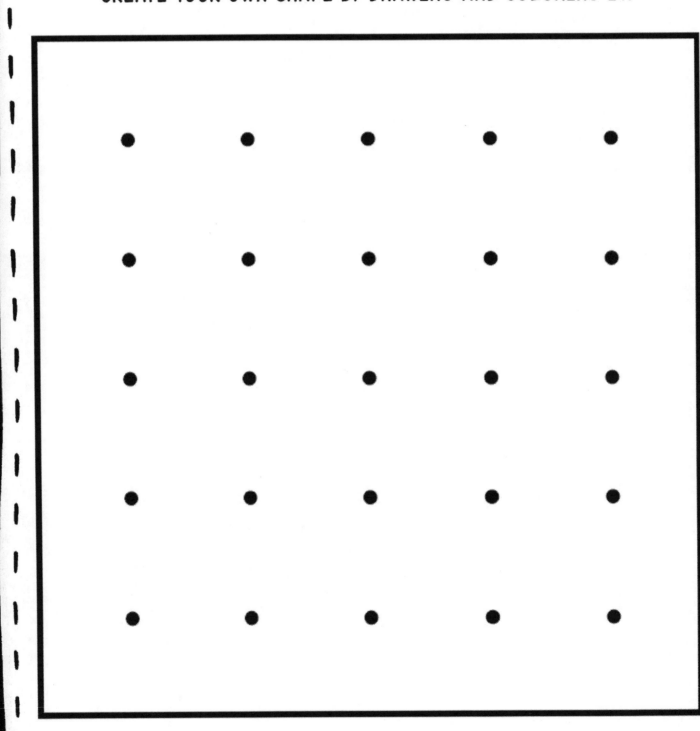

CREATE YOUR OWN SHAPE

CREATE YOUR OWN SHAPE BY DRAWING AND COLORING IT.

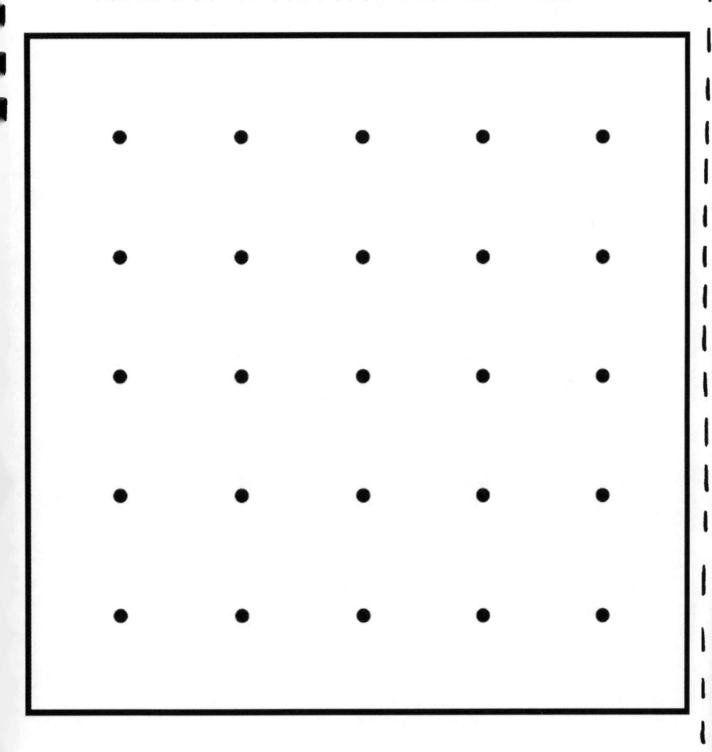

CREATE YOUR OWN SHAPE

CREATE YOUR OWN SHAPE BY DRAWING AND COLORING IT.

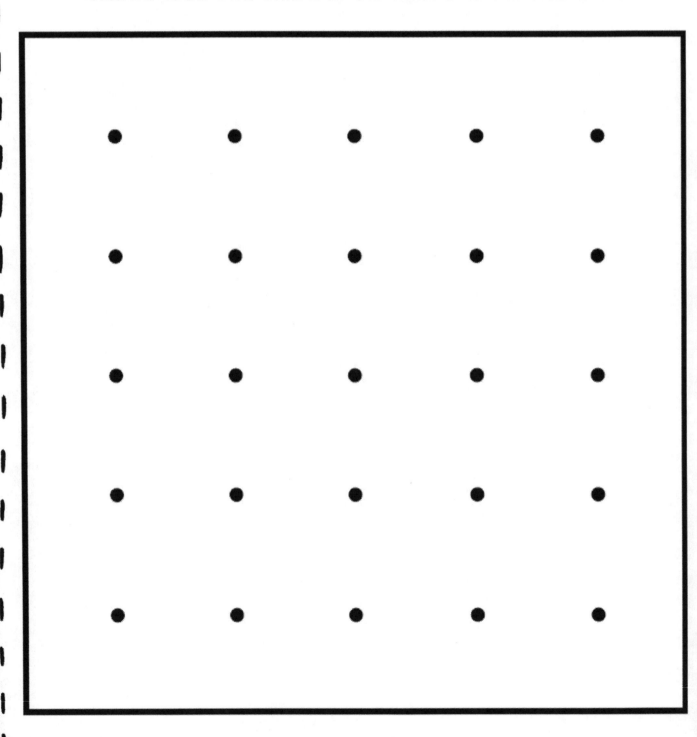

CREATE YOUR OWN SHAPE

CREATE YOUR OWN SHAPE BY DRAWING AND COLORING IT.

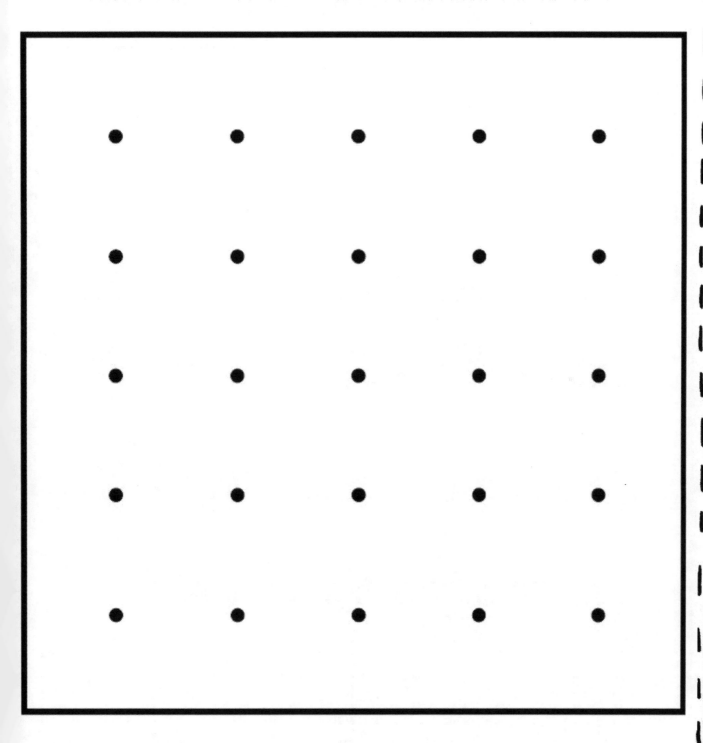

SQUARE

CIRCLE ALL THE SQUARE !

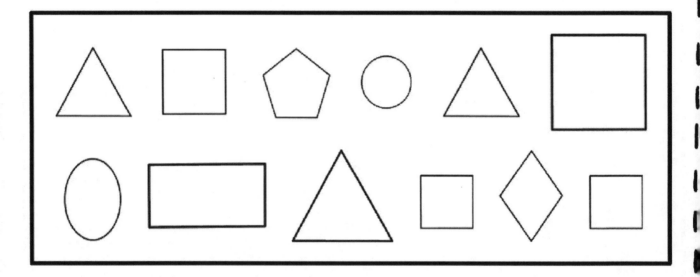

WHICH OBJECT SHAPED LIKE SQUARE

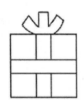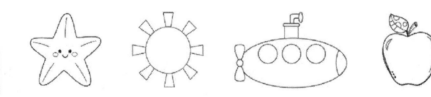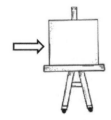

TRACE THE SHAPE BELOW

RECTANGLE

CIRCLE ALL THE RECTANGLE!

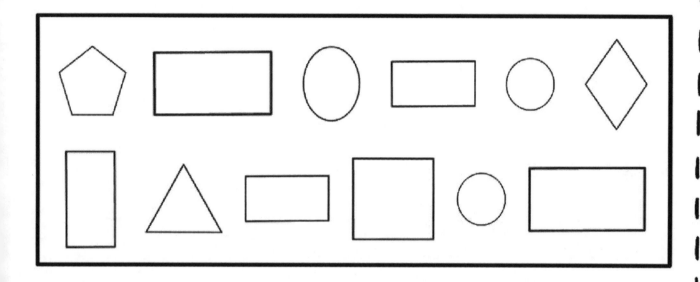

WHICH OBJECT SHAPED LIKE RECTANGLE

TRACE THE SHAPE BELOW

TRIANGLE

CIRCLE ALL THE TRIANGLE

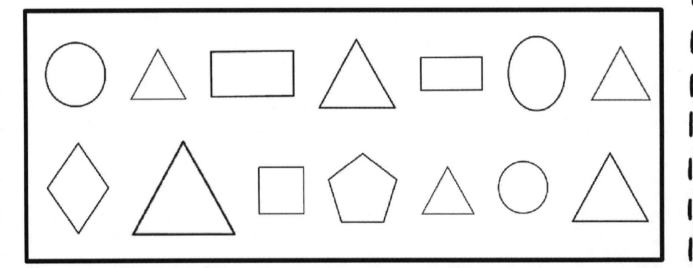

WHICH OBJECT SHAPED LIKE TRIANGLE

TRACE THE SHAPE BELOW

CIRCLE

CIRCLE ALL THE CIRCLES

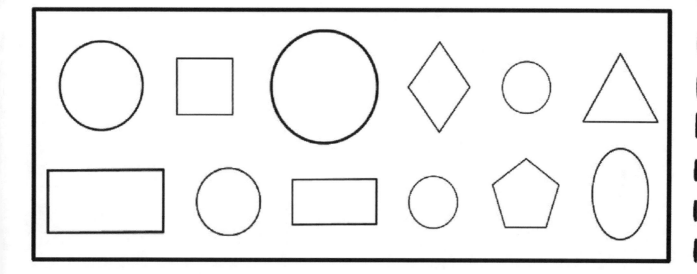

WHICH OBJECT SHAPED LIKE CIRCLE

 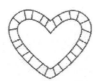 

TRACE THE SHAPE BELOW

OVAL

CIRCLE ALL THE OVALS

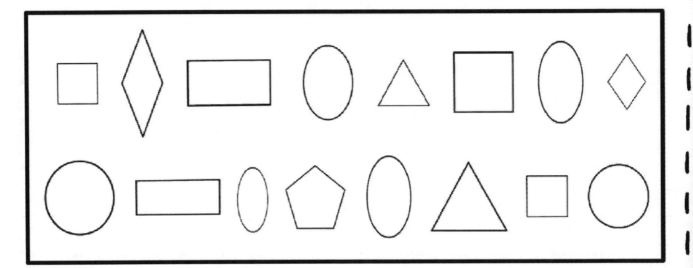

WHICH OBJECT SHAPED LIKE OVAL

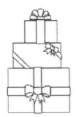    

TRACE THE SHAPE BELOW

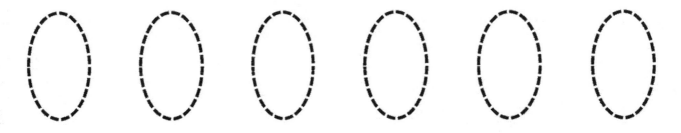

RHOMBUS

CIRCLE ALL THE RHOMBUSES

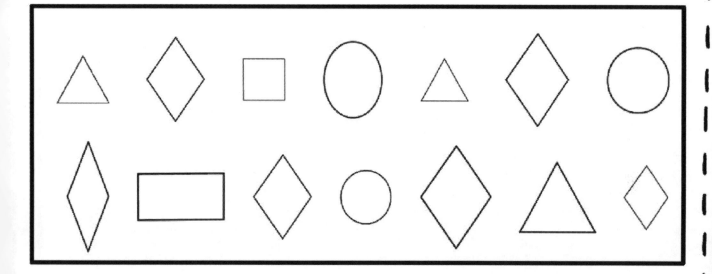

WHICH OBJECT SHAPED LIKE RHOMBUS

TRACE THE SHAPE BELOW

TRAPEZOID

CIRCLE ALL THE TRAPEZOIDS

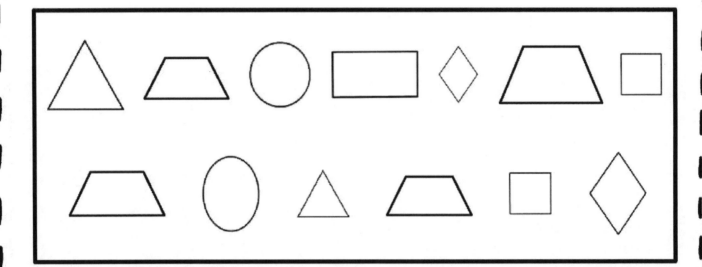

WHICH OBJECT SHAPED LIKE TRAPEZOID

     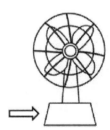

TRACE THE SHAPE BELOW

PENTAGONS

CIRCLE ALL THE PENTAGONS

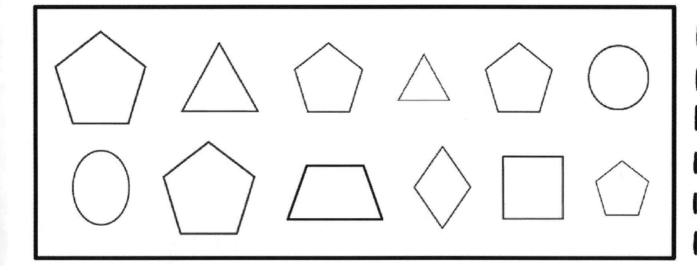

WHICH OBJECT SHAPED LIKE PENTAGON

     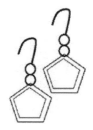

TRACE THE SHAPE BELOW

3D SHAPE

CIRCLE THE OBJECTS IN EACH ROW THAT MATCH THE SHAPE ON THE LEFT

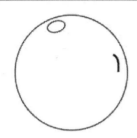 Sphere	 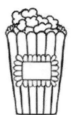  
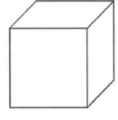 Cube	  
 Cone	→   
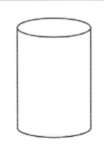 Cylinder	

42396098R00042